INVESTING MADE SIMPLE

INVESTING MADE SIMPLE

Building Wealth for the Future

ROWAN EVERHART

QuantumQuill Press

CONTENTS

1	Introduction	1
2	Setting Financial Goals	3
3	Understanding Risk	7
4	Investment Options	10
5	Building a Diversified Portfolio	14
6	Tax Considerations	17
7	Investment Strategies	20
8	Monitoring and Adjusting	24
9	Investing for Retirement	27
10	Conclusion	30

Copyright © 2024 by Rowan Everhart

All rights reserved. No part of this book may be reproduced in any manner whatsoever without written permission except in the case of brief quotations embodied in critical articles and reviews.

First Printing, 2024

CHAPTER 1

Introduction

This dissertation for investment learners explains how conservative people can systematically invest in safe government and corporate bonds. Included through the edge of "smart-beta" security acquisition strategies are equity market investments, consisting of pure, single-company shares. As an example of a better approach to safe investing, corporate obligations, business ventures, and other secure financial instruments are exchanged daily on the open market. Smart trading in fixed-income assets can help develop a substantial economic foundation for young people, even those who do not use high-risk equity assets in their investment strategies. The production of an ESG investment strategy for any stable investor included with businesses also often comprising companies begins with the investment rules found in Ecclesiastes 11:1-6, suggested of the wisest investor, Solomon himself.

Introduction: "Money grows on the tree of Edit and does not expire. Picking the fruit does not end up empty-handed." (Proverbs 10:24) The wealthiest man who ever lived, King Solomon, offers fantastic advice to young people who are just starting out in life. Lately, his economic insights have become widely accepted in the general public as well. Solomon believed that by investing almost everyone should build a large fortune. Because the accumulation of money makes life decidedly more comfortable, investing is more important than almost any other earthly pursuit. With thousands of years of confirmation that investing in virtually any business enterprise enriches mankind, King Solomon's ageless wisdom has inspired my mission to promote universal investing in the public. Every responsible child, in my opinion, should begin investing on the day he or she begins receiving an allowance.

1.1. Importance of Investing

Everyone in your family will see the value in investing. A significant benefit of investing is that it provides appreciation and capital gains on your contributed funds, not just a sense of living with enough; it promotes security in the household. Even though we are constantly bombarded with an investing message today, many can't describe what investing is, what it means, and what it achieves. People make mostly haphazard investments based on tips, news, feelings, or recommendations from others. This article presents informative essential investing information summarizing tasks and connecting related technologies that can enhance or compromise any investor's strategy.

Investing is one of the most important things you'll ever do in your life. We invest in our future and our family. Without it, there would be no higher education, housing, or future retirement. Very few people earn enough money to not worry about investing, and it is important to start young if you can. The earlier you begin, the more money you will be able to accumulate, and the more time it will have the opportunity to grow. Children learn good money habits from their parents.

CHAPTER 2

Setting Financial Goals

Think of your short-term financial goal, your long-term financial goal, and of course, your financial goals for today. Write down your years-long financial goal. Write down your today financial goal. You don't need a degree in finance to invest money. Whether your financial goals are short-term, long-term, for today, as an investor, it will benefit you to learn a few fundamental investment principles, to understand investment concepts, like asset allocation and compounding interest, and to learn how to navigate how to structure and monitor a portfolio, using apps and websites to help and as well know when to sell investments. Educated investors are informed investors and are better equipped to make smart investment decisions so know that investing is typically a marathon and not a race. Remember, financial goals meaningfully inform the investment decision-making process. When done right, investing represents a tried-and-true way to beat inflation while building wealth for the future of your financial goal. Reduced levels of paying credit card interest, and being eligible to max out emergency savings and retirement account contributions are some of the many financial benefits. In other words, when you invest, you start putting your hard-earned money to work for you, in a portfolio, on your behalf, for tomorrow's possible inflation, retirement, and individual financial goals.

Wealth advisors use the acronym SMART to help their clients set financial goals. It stands for specific (be precise about what you want to achieve), measurable (make sure you can determine when you have succeeded at your goal), attainable (be realistic so that you can figure out if the goal is achievable within the needed time horizon), relevant (your goal should make sense for your financial plan), and time-bound (set a target date for reaching your goal, including milestones along the way). For instance, saving $500,000 in an individual retirement account (IRA) for retirement in 10 years while reaching a specific retirement savings portfolio balance to protect savings so saving along the way would be a SMART financial goal. At other times, you may need money for an event happening at exactly five years away, or particular year, or for today such as to pay an annual expense. In these cases, you would adjust your goal to meet these demands, if necessary. Remember, money has time value, and in general, the sooner you start saving for your goals, the better as it becomes easier to invest.

First things first: start with the end in mind. That is, set your financial goals, or why you're investing. Perhaps you want to buy a home, to pay off student loans, to retire, to beat inflation, to save a six-month or year's emergency fund, to take an annual vacation, or to reach other personal or family financial goals. Setting financial goals is an important first step and will guide your investment decision-making process and overall investment strategy.

2.1. Short-Term vs Long-Term Goals

By investing in many different asset classes, the fear of losing one's SSI benefits may pass as one's savings and savings earnings continue to grow. Ultimately, the investor knows there is a little cushion of diversified investments that may protect him from the uncertainties anticipated in old age and declining health. Reassured of his safety net, most retirees do not consider retirement annuities or immediate or variable immediate annuities as part of the solution to their retirement savings problem.

Investment misconceptions for long-term savers. Many people find it simple to match long-term savings goals with long-term investments by investing excess savings into a "diversified investment portfolio" of stocks, corporate bonds, real estate, and commodities. The earnings from small investments may not be very large, but an opportunity does exist to earn something from their investment, regardless of their growing financial constraints.

Short-term vs long-term goals. Many people find it simple to match long-term investment goals with long-term investments by investing excess savings into a "diversified investment portfolio" of stocks, corporate bonds, real estate, and commodities. The earnings from small investments may not be very large, but an opportunity does exist to earn something from their investment, regardless of their growing financial constraints.

2.2. SMART Goal Setting

The basic rule of goal setting is that you need to have a reason to save so that you can achieve your desires. You must start by deciding what you want to achieve in life, then draw up a plan that will help you achieve your objectives and dreams. It does not help to have short term and long term goals that say "I want to go on holiday". This will take time to save for, so rather break it down and decide to save a specific amount of money per month that will help you achieve the end goal. A SMART goal could be: "I would like to save R3 000 over 12 months for holiday". You will be able to measure how much you are going to save, and when you should save it by.

Setting SMART financial goals will guide you in making good investment decisions. SMART goals are Specific, Measurable, Achievable, Relevant and Time Bound. An example of a SMART goal is: "I would like to save R500 by the end of the year so that I will be able to buy a toy for myself in December". Let us unpack that goal: Specific - the goal is clear and well defined and answers the "what", "why" and "how" of the goal. Measurable - the goal is quantifiable. In other words you will be able to measure how much progress you are making and when you have reached the goal. That brings us to Time Bound - the goal has a time limit. The "end of the year" gives it a deadline, this makes it a SMART goal.

CHAPTER 3

Understanding Risk

Market risk is the risk that your investment could lose value due to price declines in the market on which our fund focuses. Since the factors behind the price declines in that market, and therefore your investment, are often broader economic factors affecting that specific market and the larger economy as a whole, market risk is not only specific to our portfolio or funds, but is widespread as well. There can be many reasons for why a market can experience a significant price decline and market risk is generally unpredictable. Therefore, it is generally considered the highest risk of all, but it can also have the highest reward over time. Market risk is not the same as fee risk, which stems from costs associated with investment products. Market risk is also different from inflation risk, the risk of incurring a diminished purchasing power in the future.

Risk isn't investing's boogeyman - it's something that can be quantified and addressed, and is an integral part of investing. It's normal for markets to fluctuate daily, but historically, the odds of making money in the stock and bond markets are in investors' favor after longer time periods. While everyone would like to avoid risk when it comes to investing, doing so can mean that inflation may erode your spending power over time. Below, we'll dive into the three types of investment risk you should keep in mind when planning your future.

3.1. Types of Investment Risks

Fluctuations in market prices of shares and bonds might affect the market value of your investment (Realized Risk). This risk can be defined as the risk the investor bears related to the overall investments that he or she could eventually have realized. Economic and financial analysis tries to determine how realistic this or that investment project is. These theories retrieved endorse the meaning by pointing to the fact that intrinsic value does exist to any investment. When doing non-informed investments, however, investors may tend to ignore such thing. Much of the information is implicitly contained in the stock price.

As an investor, you will be exposed to trading and non-trading risks. Trading risks are linked with the fluctuation of market prices of shares and bonds as a result of day-to-day fluctuations of supply and demand existing on the market. The non-trading risks have nothing to do with adverse market price movements, but with any other factors, which can complicate your investment project. Several different non-trading risks exist for which various forms of protection measures are suggested.

3.2. Risk Tolerance Assessment

To begin, take this risk tolerance assessment to evaluate the percentage weights among the following investment categories: very conservative, conservative, moderate, aggressive and very aggressive. Your responses will be used to assess the percentage of these weightings into your portfolio of funds. Remember, "past performance is not indicative of future results." Your investment risk profile: You are a careful, cautious or conservative investor. You seek investments that offer security and relatively stable value. Your investment risk profile: You are a moderate or balanced investor. You seek investment funds that offer a mixture of principal protection, income and long-term growth consistent with the capital appreciation of assets. Your investment risk profile: You are an enterprising, willing to take some risks investor. You seek investments that provide a strong potential for long-term capital appreciation but are willing to accept temporary declines in performance value for them.

Investments are not FDIC-insured, nor are they deposits of or guaranteed by a bank or any other entity, so they may lose value. Investors should carefully consider investment objectives and risks, as well as charges and expenses of a fund or ETF before investing. This and other information are contained in the respective prospectus or the summary prospectus, which may be obtained from a financial professional and should be read carefully before investing. An investor could lose most or all of their principal; some funds have experienced periods of losses that lasted several years. There are additional risks associated with investing in individual securities tailored to a specific category or sector. Investments in emerging markets for which invested in the AdvisorShares fund may be considered speculative and are subject to more excessive market risks than investments in a diversified group of developed countries.

CHAPTER 4

Investment Options

If you are starting to invest, you should be interested in investment funds (ETF and AUM). These funds usually offer broad coverage of the market and have a lower transaction cost advantage to most mutual funds. Also, the risk of investment funds is lower than some investment vehicles and can be a diversified long-term investment option for someone who doesn't want to take the risk. Naturally, the fact that investment funds are a suitable option for most individual investors draws an extra risk to your investment tool, which is your portfolio investment. Though an investment fund can offer a broad coverage of a portfolio, the investor who wants to reduce climate and deflationary risk has to organize his investment fund as an investment with the physical distribution of assets.

Let's imagine you saved at least a certain amount of your salary as part of your new financial planning. If you are going to raise your net worth with the money you kept, you need to invest this money. In this way, it is possible to increase the amount of money you saved through time. When it comes to investing, we generally think of the stock market. We remember the stock market crashes and booms; however, the stock market is a category of investments. Financial markets offer a lot of options in which you can invest. Some of these options are a money market fidelity, treasury, investment funds (ETF – Exchange

Traded Fund and AUM - Assets Under Management), private market investments, bonds, gold, silver or other precious metals, collectibles. Moreover, you can choose the equivalent of certain assets that are not physically available.

4.1. Stocks

Every three to six months, hundreds of dollars could be put away until the worth of Jack and Jill's stocks are substantially added. Then, if money is suddenly needed, United Community Banks provides dividends for their stockholders. Stocks are supposed to be held for at least 5 years. Therefore, as long as stocks own priorities are held, a 15-year financial strategy might be awaited. Stock costs may sometimes decrease. This implies that stocks are generally ordered cheaper. Research was conducted to provide significant information regarding the 'levels of excitement' indicated by the business media. During a time in which the actual value of the stocks had the possibility to be higher when the purchase cost was cheap, entertainment or SMB was subtracted from SMB. The future substantial yields that powered investors' hopes for more costly future stock prices, pulled from the examination dataset, were also reported by journalists.

4.1. Stocks. Sufficient returns would regularly accumulate for many years, if little amounts of money were consistently put away and held in stocks. Studies show an average of 9 percent. This figure is in an exact period as number 1 several years. The average last 15 years gain for the Dow Jones Industrial Average is also 7 percent. At Vanguard, $500 is the minimum initial investment needed to cover an index fund. No one toil consider expensive stocks each time any small amount of money is saved. Stocks with a lower overall cost can be chosen instead; most firms provide funds exposed to an extensive variety of stocks. These have reduced danger for the lump sum investment due to their variety.

4.2. Bonds

Bonds are broadly classified into three groups, according to the bond issuer: Government, Municipality, and Corporate. The broad majority of government bonds are issued exclusively by countries. Countries with a low likelihood of default (think about Germany or Switzerland) usually pay lower interests to bond buyers compared to countries with a higher likelihood of default. Once this is established, corporate bonds follow similar dynamics. Large, established companies pay lower interest than small, troubled ones (which can pay obscene interest rates). When a country or a company becomes depressed, the probability of it not honoring the loan increases. Bond buyers understand this and sell their bonds requiring now higher interest payments for them. Bond prices collapse and interest rates soar. Bond prices are established by a secondary market where previously issued bonds are bought, sold, and re-bought. Bond prices and interest rates have an opposite relationship.

Bonds are the second largest asset class and its three different types capture 15% of a traditional 60/40 portfolio. Thus, they deserve some of our attention too. Bonds are loans. Two parties agree to the term, the interest rate, and the amount money in exchange for a piece of paper that formalizes the pact. The buyer of the bond is the lender and the issuer of the bond is the borrower. A bond is characterized by three key variables: Term, Credit risk, and Yield. The bond's term tells you when will your money be returned. The credit risk tells you the probability that this may not happen. The yield tells you the compensation, in annual terms, that the borrower is willing to provide. It represents a combination of the two previous variables.

4.3. Mutual Funds

Opening the Discussion on Index Funds Back in the 1970s, John C. Bogle, a prominent American investor and administrator, introduced the concept of "indexing" as a mutual fund investment strategy. Instead of an active manager overseeing the portioning of a portfolio to generate returns, surrogate niche stock indexes track macroeconomic indices. These indices consist of market sub-components or specific sub-indices that track different categories or size-ranges of investments and measure their total performance. As born in Bogle's theory, an index fund is a mutual fund called an "investment portfolio" that seeks to produce returns that exactly replicate that of various indices, such as the Standard & Poor's 500 Index. Whether or not this pure passive strategy can generate high returns is still a matter of debate.

A mutual fund is a pool of funds from many investors that is used to buy stocks, bonds, or other investment products. Because a mutual fund is made up of a combination of individual contributions, it is generally considered a collective investment, allowing investors to diversify without needing to buy a multitude of individual securities. Investors purchase shares of a mutual fund at its most current net asset value, also commonly referred to as its "NAV" per share. The NAV fluctuates continuously, depending on the prices of the financial instruments within the fund. In most cases, a mutual fund will also charge investors a redemption fee, or "back load," if they decide to sell their shares within the first five years of purchasing them. The goal of a mutual fund is to provide modest to medium long-term return, while also maintaining the safety of the investment. The concept of a mutual fund is appealing due to its more accessible and personalized nature.

CHAPTER 5

Building a Diversified Portfolio

2. Diversify your investments to reduce risk. If you've ever sat through a scary movie, then you know those most chilling parts often come in the pauses between the action. The approaching steps, the flickering lights, the expectant echoes and rumblings: they all raise the suspense. As your mind fills in the blanks, your fears grow. You don't know what will happen, but you know whatever it is will scare the heck out of you. And then, often when the terror finally appears, it's a bit of a letdown. Because now you know the monster isn't a demon; it's just Jason with a hockey mask, or Freddie with his metal nails. With that knowledge, what really scared you the most turned out to be the unknown suspense itself. That's the power of suspense and the unknown. It's why great musicians use silence and empty notes with as much effect as loud and bloated ones, and why it's better to go out with questions in your story than with none. That same principle applies to investing. Investors face a paradox: you want to be protected if the unknown terror arrives (like one of those rare market calamities); at the same time, you don't want to miss out on any of the anxious moments in less scary periods, when things are going well. How do you handle this risk-management paradox? By embracing something we're all told to hate as kids - which is why, like spinach and cod liver oil, we learned

to love it as adults. That which we dislike as kids usually does us good. And so it is with what grown-up investors - investing savants, you may call them - do: build and monitor a diversified investment portfolio.

5.1. Asset Allocation Strategies

When you want to diversify your retirement savings to reduce risk, there are other options available to consider. Diversification is an approach that uses multiple investments within a single portfolio, the goal of which is to offset – or nullify – any losses in one asset type by the gains in another asset type. Portfolio managers often diversify their investments to spread risk among many different types of investments, and manage risk and return. It's a 'let's not put all our eggs in one basket' way of taking care of wealth building. And in a retirement savings portfolio, which is focused on increasing your wealth, it's not unusual to assign a moderate to aggressive strategy that includes a high proportion of stocks.

Amy Fontinelle says the asset allocation strategy that's best for you at any given time in your life depends on two things – your age and your investment horizon, or the number of years for which you expect to be investing. Historically, investing in the stock market has been one of the best ways to increase the wealth of your future and grow your assets. But remember – there are also risks involved when you invest in stocks. Stocks can and do lose value from time to time, and in the industry, market experts say that past performance is not an indication of future returns. In other words, when the economy changes or if there's a significant decline in the stock market, stocks might not perform as well when you retire as they may have when you first began investing – and that can increase your financial risks as you near age 65.

5.2. Rebalancing Your Portfolio

If you have neglected properly rebalancing your portfolio, your risk may now be relatively high without you realizing it, particularly when markets fluctuate after you have made large additions to your stock funds. Although that heightened risk can result in high returns if things turn out well, you may need to think twice about the implications of large stock market swings on your portfolio value and rein in your investments in stock funds. In essence, the objective of rebalancing is to restore your portfolio to its original, carefully balanced or assigned mix of funds. With a process that involves at least three steps, you re-adjust the claims of your funds until they once again balance your risk against your anticipated returns. Nor is there anything magical about the 35-45 mix of stock funds for savers and retirees. If your risk tolerance should be different, you will have to come up with a mix that would work best for you with respect to balancing the risks and benefits of your investments.

When the value of your funds gets relatively high, you may want to counteract the elevated risk by selling some of those funds and channel the proceeds into the funds that have not done so well and may now be unduly underrepresented in your portfolio. This is particularly true for stock funds with their potentially fantastic returns that may be magnified in a surging stock market. By selling portions of those funds that have surged and acquiring interests in the underrepresented funds, you may also align yourself with the principle of "buying low and selling high," even if you succeed in selling your shares for more than you had paid for them.

CHAPTER 6

Tax Considerations

Before the long term capital gains tax rates of today became official in 2013, they were very different. More than a hundred years ago, in 1913, an individual could expect to be taxed up to 20%. Then for the following 68 years, expect to pay between 20% to 77% according to our ordinary income tax structure. It wasn't until the Internal Revenue Code of 1954 that this law was amended to include the $0.71 million exclusion from the previous adjusted cost basis. Afterward, investors could look forward to realizing gains at their current long term capital gains rate of 15% during the years 1954-2003. Subsequently, in 2003, the Bush tax cuts cut from 15% to 0% for those in the 10% to 15% ordinary income tax bracket, and for those in the 25-35% bracket, they were taxed 15%. After the Bush tax cuts were allowed to expire in 2013, our current LTHG tax structure of 0% to 23.8% became the effective long-term capital gains tax rates of today. How much will the tax hit you if you choose to get wealthy through earning money for spending? Our ordinary income rates, which range from 10% to 37%.

One of the greatest tax advantages in our tax code is the long term capital gains tax loophole. This allows individuals who receive capital gains from funds held for longer than a year to be taxed up to 23.8% less than those who are subject to our ordinary income tax structure. The reason for this tax break is to incentivize investment in the economy for the long term. Since most millionaires came about their fortune through investing in the stock market, this tax break plays a large part in becoming a millionaire yourself!

6.1. Tax-Efficient Investing

For instance, in 2021, if your taxable income was between $34,000 and $82,000, your effective tax rate would be 12 percent or a sum of $4,800. But on just the $34,000 to $82,000 part of your income, the actual tax rate would be, well, let's do the math: 12 percent of $82,000 = $9,840 and 12 percent of $34,000 = $4,080. $9,840 - $4,080 = $5,760. This is your marginal tax rate. So one of the loopholes in the grand tax situation is how you invest your portfolio. Assets kick off different types of income. The three most common forms of income lubrication are interest, short-term capital gains, which currently up to a year's investment, is taxed at your actual or marginal tax rate. Longer-term capital gains, or investment of more than one year at lower rates, are taxed at zero. So the very first decision that you should make is to try and minimize either your tax rate or the type of income.

Tax information is supposed to be personal. It should be based on your specific situation and yield the information that is customized to your unique circumstance. "Tax efficiency" or "tax management" are buzzwords that are used in the investment world. But what do they mean? Why are they important? Think about tax efficiency as a way of increasing your investment return by paying less in taxes. You probably should have the goal of keeping as much of the money you can that you have earned rather than giving a big chunk of it to the taxman. First, just focus on the income part of investing. There are ways to minimize your actual tax costs. We have already mentioned the effective tax rate and the marginal tax rate.

6.2. Tax-Advantaged Accounts

Remember, money contributed into a traditional 401(k) is not taxed until it is withdrawn, which should be after retirement, whereas money in a Roth 401(k) is always taxed before it is contributed. The decision to use a traditional or Roth 401(k), along with what asset allocation to pursue within a 401(k), play a central role in planning for retirement. People who anticipate that their income tax rate will be lower during retirement tend to be better suited for a traditional 401(k), as do Millennials with lower starting salaries at less than $40,000, as college graduates with lower salaries can benefit from using traditional 401(k)s to decrease taxable income, possibly boosting their eligibility for income-based loan repayment programs. Note that the deduction for traditional 401(k) contributions is not limited. On the other hand, people who believe they may increase their income over time tend to be better suited for a Roth 401(k). Keep in mind that unlike the traditional 401(k), a Roth 401(k) plan is open to high-income professionals and effectively supports their future.

By now, you should be feeling pretty good about an investment account, and that's right where you should be. Investment accounts are essential, but they aren't the final step to preparing for the future. Now we will talk about the sixth and final means to financial empowerment: tax-advantaged accounts. These accounts are wonderful in that they come with numerous tax benefits and can really elevate your retirements savings. There are several different types of tax-advantaged accounts, which mainly differ based on whether the deposits are made before taxes are taken out of them, as well as how the accounts are taxed upon withdrawal. The most popular tax-advantaged accounts, and therefore the ones we will discuss in this book, include traditional 401(k)s, pre-tax 401(k)s, traditional and Roth IRAs, and 529 college savings plans. Let's start by talking about 401(k)s.

CHAPTER 7

Investment Strategies

Some general guidelines are crucial. In the majority of cases, you should regularly review your portfolio, looking for general trends and changes. Specific events often remind investors of their need to review. Perhaps you've been planning your grandchild's education fund. Watching TV news, you see a Chinese government official proudly announce a major initiative to spur technology development. That's a signal you should research mutual funds composed of companies that may benefit. Perhaps flash and pop from electric cars interest you. After all, Elon Musk has become either a god or a devil to you. Internet chats pique your curiosity about a non-IP-driven supplier of electric battery metals — cobalt, lithium, and nickel. You can research mutual funds that hold such investments. Or perhaps the president signs a multi-trillion-dollar infrastructure bill. The advance in stock prices signals Federal Reserve higher interest rate worries. Yield on ten-year Treasuries rapidly rises. Within weeks, the tech-heavy NASDAQ 100 declines closely to 10%. These or other events often signal various segments of the economy, such as technology or commodities, are likely to grow more or less robustly.

If you're setting a portion of your hard-earned money aside for something serious, such as a child's education, retirement, or the ability to retire, you might as well try to make the most of it. In this section, you learn important stuff about investing, like caring for your portfolio; asset allocation and diversification; and time-tested portfolio strategies, such as growth, value, and income investing. You also find out about some of the favorite investment vehicles of the 21st century investor (or not) — Exchange-Traded Funds and dividend reinvestment plans. And you're privy to some hot investing strategies of today and what's in store tomorrow. Investors must carefully monitor their investment portfolios. They want their money to grow, but they also want downside risk dampened. These potentially conflicting goals help explain why professional financial planners often refer to portfolio monitoring as one of the trickiest parts of active investing.

7.1. Dollar-Cost Averaging

The most effective way to put DCA into practice is by investing a specific amount at regular intervals. This allows you to capture both the increase and the decrease in stock prices for a more consistent return within your investments. Especially during times of high market volatility, dollar cost averaging keeps price swings from dictating your investment strategy, so touch base with a financial professional to figure out the right course of action for you. Even if somebody else is managing your investments overall, there are brokerages available where a determined investor can set up and implement a specific dollar-cost averaging strategy for diversified mutual funds and Exchange-Traded Funds (ETFs). Many of the stories that we have heard are from people who are approaching retirement, starting families, or re-localizing, but dollar-cost averaging can be a great way for anyone to bolster their investment strategy.

But if a fear of losing money to a stock loss is preventing you from investing, remember, you can't lose money if you don't sell. As you buy shares of a stock at various prices over time, you take the chance of offsetting some of those highs and lows along the way, reducing the need for those super high highs to offset the lows. You will want to be mindful and invest responsibly. DCA a great approach, but is not foolproof, nor can it guarantee profits.

7.2. Buy and Hold Strategy

Having invested regularly in necessary personal expenses and other auxiliary emergencies, to avoid human emotions' influence on decision-making is the greatest test of this strategy. To ignore current share price trends, especially when it is not favorable, takes both willpower and endurance. Nevertheless, even if you have witnessed a decline in stock value up to the 75% mark, affording you the opportunity to stock up on promising blue chips whose comeback is inevitable, your comfort will relent. Indeed, history has shown that the share market has an upward bias. Once you have "your foot in the door," so to speak, this strategy is most likely to generate cash flow. Furthermore, don't focus on timing the market; rather, buy shares continuously every month. Just because it's trendy, don't buy shares when prices fall steeply or rise dramatically. For stock market investing, this rule applies as well. Recognize that a worthy purchase will create sound companies consistent with this strategy.

Also known as a "buy and forget" strategy, buying and holding shares in solid, dividend-paying companies is Warren Buffet's preferred strategy for growing financial wealth. According to the Oracle of Omaha and the third richest man in the world, stock market investing should be simple. By selecting the right companies to place your faith in, your stock portfolio should generate regular cash flow. However, to maximize the potential of dividend income, you should not use it for personal consumption but reinvest the sum back into acquiring more company shares.

7.3. Value Investing

7.3. Value Investing. The value of an investment is calculated by looking at the expected future cash flows and discounting them at a predicted interest rate over the holding period. The valuation is intrinsic, leaving aside the shares regularly bought and sold on the major stock exchange. They buy Zalando at 108 and sell it at 220, paid out 112 plus an exorbitant profit. The valuation of an investment, which everyone here calls intrinsic value investing, is to sum up all future expected cash flows generated by the financial investment over the holding period, subjecting each individual cash flow to an applicable discount. The sum calculated in this way must be higher than the price paid for the share or shares for the investment to be made, provided that the risk profile of the investment meets one's own investment policy.

Hey, you may be thinking. What is value investing and what has it got to do with me? What it means - believe it or not - is no more than buying what is cheap and stocking it in your own financial stock kitchen. Then you can take advantage of the value investing meal every month. Instead of speculating that fast-growing companies should increase in value every year, holding the company stock and letting the investment compound apparently benefits you as a value investor, because what is cheap will become more expensive when inflation is on the rise. But first things first. As described earlier, value investing or intrinsic value is by no means a new idea but even an old, red-light idea that Henry Scott used back when that sometimes old rascal Dick Turpin charged passing ships and robbed their insecurely stuffed treasures. What he did regularly every year, often on a Sunday afternoon outside Walthamstowe.

CHAPTER 8

Monitoring and Adjusting

Investment plan adjustments can occur at the conclusion of the annual review. Monitoring the investment portfolio is also an ongoing activity. Timely financial decisions may be made when faced with portfolio rebalancing issues, tax obligations, or even a change in the investor's situation. Monitoring will allow for corrective actions. The major impetus for monitoring the portfolio is keeping it on track with the financial objectives and policy. Individuals without an investment plan or strategy may not have a course of action when faced with a new financial situation such as the need to liquidate a portion of their portfolio assets. Reevaluation then becomes necessary.

Evaluation takes place on an ongoing basis. Some individuals are inclined to take a casual approach to investment portfolio evaluation. Part of a portfolio's investment strategy should include an evaluation of investment decisions. The process should not focus on portfolio performance alone. A portfolio evaluation should include qualitative and quantitative analyses. Aspects to evaluate include the composite performance of investment decisions (bundling similar types of investments made within a specific period such as X number of mutual fund investments). The performance evaluation should include an understanding of investment decisions' terms which affect the analysis (e.g., contributions, withdrawals, and compounded growth) rather than solely reviewing the numbers.

8.1. Tracking Performance

To quickly sum up this, we can say that when the economy is doing well, during bull markets, and when assets are doing well, shift funds out of these assets and into fixed income assets. This is performed to protect principal when markets start to collapse. However, when the economic cycle turns and starts to recover from bear markets, these funds will then be shifted back into risky assets in order to sell fixed income assets to fund equity investments. Rebalancing can be performed by using different strategies, for example. You can allocate 40% into equity investments and 60% into fixed income investments. However, different asset classes have different riskiness and expected returns over the risk. Risky assets offer higher expected returns, but with a higher risk of potential loss.

First, find the current weight of assets in your investment profile. Second, find the target weight of assets according to your investment profile. Third, subtract 1 from the other for each asset to calculate the percent of actual and target weights. Fourth, estimate the overall fund divided by the actual asset percent. Fifth, subtract the total invested fund in a certain asset. Sixth, sum up all invested funds and financed from each asset. This is then your fund needed for each sector if brought into balance. The fund needed can now be used to decide whether you should buy or sell as much into each asset to achieve balance.

One of the most important activities to keep in mind after your initial investments is to track the performance of your investments. In most cases, the performance of your investments will impact how your portfolio looks in the future. It is important to track your investments, and it is just as important to not let any emotions interfere with the buy or sell decision process. Normally, rebalancing is done about twice a year.

8.2. Making Changes as Needed

A simple way of finding cheap annuities is to phone several brokers to compare the quotes and ask if there are any other annuities with better rates. Ideally, you will be offered the best rate available in the nation. I never thought that I would be able to retire when I wanted; however, I only needed to save about 30% of what I was saving to get to my retirement goals. In Paul Farrell's The Lazy Person's Guide to Investing, you can find some really simple rules. You should routinely check them. Not only will you find cheaper annuities, but you may also find better alternatives for your IRAs and brokerage accounts. You should also look at the power of the AAA stocks, how much you will have if you invest in these AAA stocks, what you need? The most important factor to consider is how much we will need to save. While you cannot possibly know how much you will need, you will have a good idea. First, what is your Social Security benefit?

When you retire, the goal is to switch from aggressive and conservative investments to a mixture of conservative and some aggressive. You want to have mostly safe investments with only a small part as risky. Zero percent risky investment is no longer a valid option. A small amount will enhance your returns. Once in retirement, use a fee-only certified financial planner to determine how to invest your money so that you will not outlive it. The Treasury Department wants us to create a safe withdrawal rate so that, for example, if you retire at age 65, you will not outlive your money if we create a private pension plan from Social Security and your retirement funds. In reality, this is impossible as different people have different life expectancies. I plan on either breaking even (no real returns after inflation) or preserving only 80% of my capital, and I play it by ear retiring after the age of 65. I also plan on most people working until the age of 80 if they have jobs. This simplifies the calculation considerably. If you ever need to get $2,000 but only have $1,800 saved for the month, you need to put the extra $200 from your risky investments aside. For this reason, it does not make sense to have all of your investments in a conservative fund if you get these deficits often.

CHAPTER 9

Investing for Retirement

You stockpile an account of consumption called bank savings that someone else is asked to use judiciously to support you, even when you no longer have the capability to earn as much as you currently do. The insurance company invests your deposit in a broad range of long-term financial instruments, some of which may be funded by companies to give you the ability to work and earn money in the future. The investment actually helps drive some of your ultimate resolve at the retirement date. Some savings may also help new startups or new business projects. A small fraction of your bank savings is allocated to these investment projects of commercial enterprises.

9. Investing for retirement. Retirement investing is an extravagant way of declaring that you are failing to live in the moment. It is also one of the simplest concepts of building a financially secure future. If you have any immediate income and you need or want equivalent income in the future, you need some way to defer the purchase of consumption goods. That's investing in a nutshell—turning current wealth into future consumption power. So you invest some money by binding your wealth in an insurance policy that protects for some uncertain future event, effectively making the money illiquid for some time period (the policy term). By signing the insurance contract—a financial instrument, you are asking a society of people who have excess consumption capacity

to lend you some support when you no longer can fully support your living costs.

9.1. Retirement Account Options

A Roth IRA is another option. With a Roth, contributions are made with after-tax dollars. The money inside the account then grows tax-free. Ideally, you want to pay the taxes on the contributions and let them grow in the tax-free account to maximize the benefit of investing within a Roth IRA. However, if your income surpasses the limit for a Roth IRA, you may not be able to open one. If you're able, it's a great account to explore. As long as you wait until a certain age to take the money, the contributions you made to a Roth IRA can be withdrawn at any time without tax or penalty. This means that you have the flexibility to tap the account for emergency expenses if needed and not worry that you'd pay a hefty penalty for doing so.

A retirement account, as the name implies, is an account specifically designed to save money for retirement. There are a few different types of retirement accounts, including ones that are opened individually and others specifically designed for small businesses. More on each type of retirement account in Chapter 9, but the two most common are a traditional IRA and a Roth IRA. With a traditional IRA, any contributions are tax deductible on your taxes that year, even if you also have a company retirement account. This can reduce your tax bill and leave with some extra cash to invest in addition to the retirement savings you're accruing. The money in your traditional IRA then grows tax-deferred. You have to pay taxes on the contributions and the earnings inside of the account when you take distributions in retirement. To open one, you don't have to have your own business; you can open an IRA through most brokerage firms.

Investing made simple: Building wealth for the future.

9.2. Planning for Retirement Income

Retirement planning is, fundamentally, an income problem. So let's go back to the concept of an annuity. What does an annuity do? It takes a pile of money and turns it into a smooth paycheck, for life, no matter how long you live. In a perfect world, we would all have an annuity from birth and would work exactly as long as we felt like it, and no longer. Then when we reached retirement age, the annuity would do all the heavy lifting. We're not in that world. Very few people actually own an annuity, because they're expensive. But an annuity is a good jumping-off point for understanding how much money you need, or how much design work you have in front of you in the years leading up to retirement. It gives us a clear way to see what you need to replace. Your goal before retirement is to set up such a stable process on your own money such that your own annuity can secure your living standard from that point forward.

What's that? So you finally made it to retirement and now, gasp, you don't have a paycheck showing up on your porch. And you don't want to go back to work. Or you're starting to think about retirement and want to know what you're working towards. Signs you've sufficiently grasped the concepts of the last chapters include starting to run the numbers on this situation. Your goal when you plan for retirement is to arrange your investments in such a way that you can safely live off them for the rest of your life. You want to arrange things such that you can get, as close as you can manage, to a smooth paycheck showing up on your porch. So, how much investment money do you need to accomplish that?

CHAPTER 10

Conclusion

Please keep in mind that regardless of your personal financial situation, full ownership of your investment, both long-term and significant savings, definitely increases the probability of a more financially secured future. The three options listed in long-term financial strategies in Chapter 1 are naturally recommended. Unlike the issuer advised by your financial advisor, also into their retirement. Thank you for taking the time to read and invest in your financial future with my e-book. Constructs and financial events are vital to personal finance advisability due to the performance of the "financial market", meaning the expected long-term returns. Keep investing in a protected, well diversified stock market index funds buy and provide yourself with an excellent lifestyle while leaving a legacy for your advisors.

As you've read throughout this e-book, the way to approach investing is very simple: to get rich, focus on meeting the investment performance of the professionals. How do we know their performance? Look at the long-term returns of market-index investments and Vanguard's annual returns. So let me say again, investing isn't some complex formula that requires manual type calculations to solve. It's just buying a few index funds, holding them for a long time, and spending time with your family and friends. No time should be regularly allocated to investing and managing financial affairs. Every day is not, every week, every month, and Monday is not stressful, although this concept often suggested by the investing industry when marketing. Ways to make money in education and long-term investment strategies are simple, money-free or low-risk. However, any investing options that try to earn instant wealth (e.g., day trading, investing in recent high-performing products, gambling) with little financial education tend to promise in the short-term risks and effort. After reading this book, please take the time to reflect your current spending habits and your long-term investment strategies. If you find that the time spent scavenging about finances has caused much stress or is often time consuming, consider adjusting your spending habits and investment strategies.

Milton Keynes UK
Ingram Content Group UK Ltd.
UKHW030908271124
451618UK00011B/338